Poetic F

MW00895568

Edited by Cynthia Sharp

May 11 2015

Dear Parvin:

Thank you for your encouragement & friendship

True
Love

Teresa Leagarke

Copyright © 2015 Cynthia Sharp

All rights reserved. No part of this book may be reproduced without written permission. All copyrights to poems belong to the individual writers.

ISBN: 1508888019
ISBN-13: 9781508888017

Acknowledgements & Credits

Wendy Bullen Stephenson: Editing Assistance & Consultation
Bee Kapitan: Web Design & Consultation
Dianne Maguire: Title & Editing
Cynthia Sharp: Literary Editor
Sharon Sharp: Nutritional Information, Recipe Research & Cooking Tips
Drew Taylor: Editing Assistance
Susan Wellisch: Project Development

With immense gratitude to all of the writers who contributed their work,
time & support.

Part of the proceeds from *Poetic Portions* will be donated to a youth scholarship fund. Each year, Pandora's Collective awards a scholarship to a young writer who shows exemplary skill level and class participation. Scholarships are either enrolment into The Vancouver Public Library's Summer Book Camp for children or teens, or enrolment into a college level creative writing course for young adults. Recipients are selected from over three hundred workshop attendees each year. "Promoting the Arts that Inspire the World to Take Notice of Itself," Pandora's Collective strives to provide a safe and inspiring environment for writers and readers of all ages. Pandora's Collective is a registered charity established to promote literacy and self-expression in Metro Vancouver, BC, Canada.

Table of Contents

Bread & Breakfast

Written on a Brown Paper Bag
by David Helwig

Sunday breakfast: the morning thinkers
stare at the pattering drops in puddles.
The yellow fire hydrant stands
rigid like a small mystic receiving truth.

Rain-slick, moodily attentive
in the downpour, the orange-green,
red-yellow taxis turn the corner
from expectation to attachment.

An orange sign declares Pizza Pizza
to the ceremonial passage of black
umbrellas. Above, a weaving of streetcar wire
delineates itself against the clouds.

Bare-legged girls pass, in shining
wet plastic. Somewhere the homeless
with their following of quiet dogs
seek whatever shelter may be.

The bread I live on. The eternal recipe with variations. Pour two cups of moderately hot water, a handful of yeast dissolved in one, a tablespoon or so of honey and a teaspoon of salt dissolved in the other, a little oil added. Add flour, half whole wheat, half white, until the stirring spoon won't stir, then knead it until its texture is smooth. Let it rise for two hours. Punch it down and put the dough in a loaf pan. Let it rise for half an hour. Bake at 350° Fahrenheit for an hour. Cool on a rack. Eat it. The same old recipe. Nothing fancy. Our daily bread.

Snow Picnic in Stanley Park
by Wendy Bullen Stephenson

Cold, wet stretches give birth to pre-season sunny days
conveying hope, optimism, and resolve.
I dare that invitation to you, Erika –
an end-winter picnic in the park.
A reconciliation?
But at morning's light, at the edge of Lost Lagoon,
paths bordered with crocuses, heather, and daffodils
are obscured by snow
silently descending like cherry petals
alighting on empty benches near deserted tennis courts.
Both restrained and self-conscious,
we struggle with how to reach across our hurts
as we tramp back toward Second Beach
aiming to reach the small pavilion to build a fire.
From the trunk of the car I fetch the "cooler"
and carry it into the shelter, which we have to ourselves.
I take out my asparagus and cheese frittata
wrapped in towels to retain the heat.
We long to set aside our regrets
and start anew. Don't we, Er?
You wipe the table's surface and set dishes on the cloth
while I light my trusty backpacking stove.
Sitting within the small circle of warmth created by the flame
is so bonding.
The frittata, fresh-from-the-oven sour cream biscuits, and carrot salad
seem tastier than ever—don't they?
And the hot apple cider from the thermos is calming.
I turn on my MP3 player, stand up, and offer you my hand
to dance together enwrapped in my opened ski jacket.
Sharing the earbuds, we move as one body to the slow music
It feels so good to be close again in our private world.
With the water reaching a boil, we step apart
as I pour the bubbles over the tea in our cups.
Extending my jacket again, I say, "Until it steeps."
When we sit down to sip, cupping bare hands
around warm mugs,
we linger over squares of dark chocolate.
In ambling toward the seawall, we try to use words,
to soothe, clarify, and reassure.
My arm around your shoulder, we look toward the horizon.
Our faces feel the warmth of each other.

Our mouths touch.
To the song of one lone lark in a leafless tree,
we kiss, giving in to something beyond ourselves.

Vegetarian Frittata (crustless quiche)

Makes 4 to 6 portions.

Ingredients:

1 small onion (about ½ cup)
1 cup grated cheddar cheese
1 or more green vegetable, such as asparagus, zucchini, broccoli, or green beans
⅓ cup slivered, blanched almonds (optional)
1 whole egg
3 egg yolks
¼ teaspoon salt
¼ teaspoon dry mustard
¼ teaspoon cayenne
¼ teaspoon nutmeg
1 teaspoon Worcestershire sauce (or more to taste)
¼ teaspoon fresh black pepper
¾ cup whipping cream
¾ cup homogenized milk
¼ cup Gruyère cheese

Directions:

• Preheat the oven to 350° F.
• Grease a 9-10 inch baking dish or pie plate at least one inch deep with vegetable oil.
• Sauté onion in oil until soft.
• Scatter this on bottom of baking dish and then cover with grated cheddar cheese
• Arrange on top of this, one or more green vegetable (just barely cooked) and almonds.
• For ease of cutting frittata after baking, arrange asparagus or green beans, etc. as if they are spokes of a wheel radiating from the centre of baking dish.
• In a small bowl beat together with egg beater or whisk: 1 whole egg, egg yolks (OK if a little of their whites go in), salt, dry mustard, cayenne, nutmeg, Worcestershire sauce (or more to taste) and fresh black pepper.
• Scald whipping cream and homogenized milk and then slowly beat into egg mixture.
• Pour over filling. Then, sprinkle evenly with gruyere.
• Bake 10 minutes at 350° F, then reduce heat to 325° F to bake 25 minutes longer or until golden, risen, and firm to touch. If top is golden but centre

is not firm enough, continue baking covered with a brown paper bag to keep top from getting too dark.

Note: some additional setting occurs after removed from oven.

To make this into a quiche, put all of the above into an uncooked crust (cooled) or precooked at 425° F for 10 minutes. Brush bottom of crust with egg white and edge of crust with egg yolk. Then bake at 325° F for 25 minutes, as above.

Either as frittata or quiche, cool slightly before serving.

Colours to Nourish the Soul
by Caroline de Chavigny

A dark grey sky, a dreary day;
Spirits are low, my smile melts away
Frozen white Earth, coldness inside
Dull wintry chills, dampness, and ice
With no end in sight, no light today
Spirits wander to a brown sandy beach
Sunsets ablaze with bold vibrant light
Of dark ruby reds and sassy bright orange
A lush forest green; a soft yellow sun
Majestic, fluorescent colours of the earth
Dancing colours of the sky, soaring high
Taking flight
Rejuvenating; nourishing my soul with life
And love, joyful sight
Fairy Princess of the Rainbow Smiles
Come back to stay

The Colours of Quiche

Ingredients:

2 deep dish pie shells
8 eggs
1 pint of heavy whipping cream
1 sassy orange carrot, shredded
1 soft yellow onion, finely cut
1 cup of fresh, ruby red cranberries, whole, cut in half
2 teaspoons of finely cut garlic
1 cup of light brown mushrooms cut in small pieces
1 cup of forest green asparagus cut in small pieces
1 cup of grated Gruyère cheese
½ cup of goat cheese
1 sprig of fresh rosemary
2 teaspoons of pepper

Directions:

- Preheat the oven to 350° F
- cover the crusts 2 deep dish pie shells with tin foil
- In a large bowl, mix until creamy:
    8 eggs
    1 pint of heavy whipping cream
- Add the following ingredients to the mixture:
    1 sassy orange carrot, shredded
    1 soft yellow onion, finely cut
    1 cup of fresh, ruby red cranberries, whole, cut in half
    2 teaspoon of finely cut garlic
    1 cup of light brown mushrooms cut in small pieces
    1 cup of forest green asparagus cut in small pieces
    1 cup of grated Gruyere cheese
    ½ cup of goat cheese, blend it in
    1 sprig of fresh rosemary
    2 teaspoon of pepper

- Mix well. Evenly spoon the mixture into the pie shells and pop in oven for 45-50 minutes. This quiche comes out light and fluffy every time and the cranberries add a really nice pop.

Tender Tiers
by Teresa-Lee Cooke

Pomegranate

      Peel away the leathery coat

Rewarded by

        jewels of red and black

            shimmering, succulent seed.

Onion

        Paper thin, parchment dry protected

Peel away the layers

        Search for the heart

           many tears later.

Peeled away

      Look

Till there was nothing

         but the tears

and the lingering aroma

The layers

      The onion

        Gone.

Onion and Blue Cheese Flatbread

Ingredients:

2 tablespoons olive oil
6 medium onions, thinly sliced
Salt to taste
3 tortillas whole wheat (9 inch)
1 tablespoon chopped rosemary (fresh)
3 ounces crumbled blue cheese
Freshly ground pepper to taste

Directions:

• Preheat oven to 400° F (200° C).
• Heat olive oil in a large skillet over low to medium heat.
• Add sliced onions and stir until they are evenly coated with oil. Sprinkle with salt. If the onions stick to the pan, add a bit of water if needed, a tablespoon at a time.
• Cook onions until the sugars in the onions caramelize (about 25–30 minutes). Stir gently with a wooden spatula to keep onions from sticking and also to mix the sugars together, as this is what browns and caramelizes the onions.
• Spread the caramelized onions onto the tortilla. Sprinkle with rosemary. Then sprinkle the crumbled blue cheese on top and season with freshly ground black pepper.
• Bake the tortillas until crisp and cheese is melted – approximately 12 minutes. Serve hot.

Note: This is best served as soon as possible after baking. The flatbread tends to get soggy the longer it sits.

Soups & Salad

The Key of N from *Glossary of Musical Terms*
by rob mclennan

Dividends, bewildered powers. Stretch-marks, nursery. Secondary heart-
beat. Listen: blood pools, pulse, the powdered structure. Spilling forth.
Grammatic, slowness. Slowness of the ground, the passage, seasons' fall.
Belonging to. Fragments, disappear. The sun sometimes divides, a music
Pressure points. Take pleasure in, a run-on, run-off. Sentenced. Is the
theme of voice. Montage, a vessel. What, you hold her. Listen, pulse.
Attention, all. As if to recognize.

rob's summer gazpacho

Ingredients:

4 Roma (plum) tomatoes, quartered
1 large cucumber, peeled and halved
½ onion, peeled and halved
½ cup green bell pepper, diced
2 (4 ounce) jars diced pimento peppers, drained
1 large can tomato juice
2/3 cup olive oil
2/3 cup red wine vinegar

Directions:

• In a blender, combine tomatoes, cucumber, chopped onion and green bell pepper, the pimento and ½ the tomato juice. Blend at high speed for 30 seconds to puree the vegetables.
• In a large bowl, mix the pureed vegetables with remaining tomato juice, olive oil and vinegar. Stir slowly for a few minutes.
• Cover mixture and refrigerate until it is well chilled (about 2 hours).
• During this time, feel free to open a bottle of red wine (any vintage). Have yourself a glass of wine.
• Serve soup in chilled bowls. Sit outside, if possible. Have another glass of wine.

Colouring
by Nicole Scoffield

I've been rambling down a winding road
Traveling trying to find my soul
As I'm wandering did I take a wrong turn?
& I'm wondering what I've learned...

Well I know on a grey day there can be rainbows
See through the blank page sunshine through the clouds
I'm staying inside the corners of my mind
Inside to colour, I'll colour outside the lines.

We're all chasing some dream, seeking some kind of peace
But in the end we have to fit in with society
Try to find harmony as we travel towards destiny
Dissonance & chaos will always be reality.
I'm going somewhere... I know it's out there
All I gotta do is get down in this rocking chair

Cause I know on a grey day there can be rainbows...

Creamy Summer Vegetable Stew
(Inspired by my best friends' gardens)

Ingredients:

2 squashes
1 large onion
1 small sweet potato
1 small yam
1 large carrot
2 sticks of celery or fennel
1 to 2 teaspoons coarse salt
½ teaspoon fresh pepper corns
¼ teaspoon cayenne pepper
½ teaspoon fennel seed
¼ teaspoon cumin seed
½ teaspoons each of fresh or dried sage and thyme
1 teaspoon turmeric
2 cloves of chopped fresh garlic
¼ teaspoon dried sea kelp
4 cups (minimum) water or organic vegetable broth

1 litre of goat's milk
1-2 ears of corn (optional)
Pre-cooked organic white or black beans (optional)
Fresh chopped tomatoes, basil and parsley

Directions:

• Pre-bake in the oven or microwave 2 of your favourite squashes & let cool. (I really like acorn and butternut squashes. Spaghetti squash is also fun – whatever suits your fancy.)
• While you precook and cool the squash…
• Dice the onion, sweet potato, yam, carrot and two sticks of celery or fennel.
• Sauté the diced vegetables on medium heat in your favourite oil such as olive or coconut oil.
• While they are cooking, separate the meat of the squash from the seeds and skin.
• Crush all the spices into a mortar & pistol, then add into the diced vegetables.
• While the vegetables and spices sauté…
• Add in the cooked squash and cover the mixture with your choice of water or organic vegetable broth, enough to cover the vegetables.
• Let the mixture simmer for 20 minutes, then add goat's milk.
• Salt to taste if needed, remembering that the soup will get saltier the longer it reduces.
• Let the soup simmer for at least another half hour to an hour before serving.
• If corn is in season, add an ear or two just before serving, as an additional sweet texture.
• If you want it to really feel like a meal, you may also add pre-cooked organic white or black beans, which add to the protein value of this hearty stew.
• Garnish with any combination of fresh chopped tomatoes, basil and parsley.
• Serve with gluten-free toast or gluten-free pasta noodles and live music.
• Enjoy!

Snowstorm
by Rogr Lee

Today it snows.
A whirling, blustering blizzard blows
Here in paradise, the first day of May..!
I float as I do,
On wheels one and two,
Down and through
A canopy of petals,
The hail of sugary blossoms
Set wild and free
By a gust of cool spring breeze.
Snowdrifts,
Fluttery pink pillows and billows
And I think of a sudden mythic
Celebration – is it?
Petals strewn, fragrance flown,
Confetti thrown and blown
Like laughter and lace
By the handfuls –
A wedding!
The smell of spring so ample,
The smell of Love – True I'm betting!
A snowstorm for summer to see
That she is the up-and-comer!
Make way!
Hand in hand, music cascading,
With only the sound of air,
Of wind, of songbirds and simple things
Parading in front of
The beginning of love
For the first time –
Full and weighty,
Light and mighty.

JAzz Cooking. My way of life.

For example, BORSCHT

Ingredients:

Vegetables of choice (Don't forget the beets and cabbage!)
Broth
Dill weed
Salt
Pepper
Sage
Thyme
Rosemary
Several tablespoons of cider or malt vinegar
Dollop of yoghurt
A handful of fresh parsley

Directions:

• Cut up the vegetables you like.
• Now, sauté each vegetable *separately* in a pat of butter or a tablespoon of olive oil.
• One by one, the vegetables will go into the pot.
• Add broth of choice, enough to cover the vegetables.
• Add dill weed, salt and pepper, sage/thyme/rosemary, if you like.
• Add a couple tablespoons of cider or malt vinegar.
• Boil, simmer, and eat. With a dollop of yoghurt. And a handful of fresh parsley.

(Oh and borscht, like many things, is even better the next day!)

Healing Hearts
By Marc Mullo

Only we can stop the persistent damaging pain,
Utter political upheaval just prolongs the bitter strain,
Returning some sense of normalcy with a gift of life,
Perhaps helping to ease the reality of continued strife,
Letting Mother Earth know that we hear her calls of disdain,
Actions will forever speak louder and clearer than just words,
Nonsensical trials and tribulations are literally idiotic and absurd,
Eventually a new sense of relief can aid the fruitful consternation,
Together anything is possible in a world of hope and distinct vision!

Gifts of the Earth Healing Salad
To nourish the mind, body and soul

Generously serves 4

It's best to grow one's own organic ingredients or obtain them at a farmer's market, and any fresh variations of local produce will work wonderfully. Ingredients have been chosen for their nutritional value, anti-depressant qualities and colour.

Ingredients:

A 5 ounce container of Earth Bound herb pre-washed salad
½ container of Earth Bound pre-washed kale
1 diced tomato
½ chopped cucumber
4 pieces chopped broccoli
1 small avocado (peeled and chopped)
1 yellow bell pepper
Shredded purple cabbage (¼ cabbage)
Shredded carrots (½ a large carrot)
¼ cup walnuts
¼ cup blueberries (wild if possible for the smaller size and increased flavour)
Organic virgin olive oil
Organic balsamic vinegar

Directions:

- Pour salad and kale into a large wooden bowl, tearing into small pieces.
- Wash and chop other vegetables.
- Scoop avocado out from the shell and peel cucumber and carrot.
- Compost peels & recycle plastic salad container.
- Add chopped vegetables, the shredded ingredients and most of the blueberries and walnuts.
- Toss the salad.
- Sprinkle with remaining walnuts and blueberries.
- Mix organic olive oil with balsamic vinegar in a 3:1 ratio for a lovely dressing. If the whole salad will be eaten immediately, the dressing can be added in before tossing, but if there might be leftovers, then it's best to let guests add their own dressing and store the components separately.

Dinner

Sweet Potato Hummus
by Honey Novick

More exquisite than you'll ever know
Gorge-o-licious from the get-go
Sweet potato hummus is nutritious
Sweet potato hummus is delicious.

Making this hummus is easy as a breeze
So here is a recipe that aims to please.
Bake sweet potatoes until they're soft,
Peal the skins off and the aroma will waft.
Mash them up with sesame tahini
Stirring it up like a Hawaiian wahini
Cut up green onions and add to the blend
Sprinkle enough garlic powder but don't offend
Add soy sauce in lieu of salt
The colour will change and the flavour will vault
Your taste buds into heaven

When adding lemon juice, the texture is moussed
But don't add too much or it'll be obtuse (and sour)
Last but not least, freshly chopped dill
The experience is guaranteed to thrill and fulfill

Scoop Sweet Potato Hummus on a pita wedge
What a wonderful way to eat and "vedge"
Friends in a circle, eat this dip
Wearing warm smiles, it makes ya feel hip.
The hipper you feel, the less you'll be a hurrier
The more you'll want to tarry, sittin' on your derriere,
Sweet Potato Hummus makes life feel merrier.

Tofu Stew Rap
by Honey Novick

Tofu Stew is what I'm making with you,
And this is what we're going to do.
Heat the pan with a little bit of oil,
Not too much or it's going to broil.
Cut up garlic and onion small
Sauté them until they enthrall.
Add carrots, tomatoes, et al
But add them later when we've done it all.

Pour some water and bouillon in the pan
Watch as it browns and wait till it boils.
Cut tofu into small chunks
Then boil it up like meatless hunks.

Add some parsnips cause they taste real sweet.
Yukon Gold potatoes are such a treat.
Include noodles of bean vermicelli
They look like glass and fill up your belly.

When everything you want is in the pan,
Cook awhile, smile awhile
Spice it up or rice it up.
Smell the flavour and taste its savour
Taste till you crave
All that goes into
Tofu Stew.

"Tofu Stew" was first published in *The Literary Gourmet* and *Fireweed*.

Spring's First Eve
by Wendy Morris

In the silent solitude of spring air,
moonlight bathing under the teasing twinkle of stars,
the sanctuary of Mom's quilt wraps me,
as my feet cool on night cedar.
Flashes of light fall as quickly as they appear.
The river's stillness is briefly interrupted
by a muskrat swimming back to bed.
A bird sings a too early morning song
and silence returns.
My eyes fill with wonder,
as contentment seeps into my soul.
The filling moon beckons me
to welcome spring's awakening
and to hear the fullness
in the silence of the Earth Mother
before she blooms into life.

Layered Organic Veggie Zucchini

Organic Ingredients:

Zucchini
Garden tomatoes
Spinach
Mushrooms
Peppers
Cottage cheese or ricotta
Mozzarella
1 can of salt-free diced tomatoes
Oregano
Garlic powder
Onion powder

Directions:

• Slice veggies thin; slice zucchini lengthwise into slender slices.
• Layer zucchini, then sliced tomatoes, cottage cheese or ricotta, then mozzarella.
• Sprinkle with oregano, garlic powder, and onion powder.
• Add more layers of veggies, along with the diced tomatoes and juice, repeating with cheese on top.
• Finish with mozzarella on top.
• Bake at 350° F for 20 minutes, or until the cheese is lightly browned.
• Serve hot.

Where did the Robins Go?
by Bonnie Nish

Where I come from
in the middle of an Eastern city
you knew when the robins in pairs
began to peck at the dirt
the first bud on the maple tree was going
to fall into your hand and burst open the earth.
Robins made life predictable, caught on paper
they remind us this is enough.

For years in this new town,
I wondered how I would know
spring had arrived without robins.
Now other things are certain.
The cherry blossoms
that line my street, crocuses that bloom in February
and when the sun cracks a partial early smile
at the world, I look out my back door
check for coyotes, then walk my dog
into morning May mist.
The crows attack my neighbour
running to catch her bus,
babies nested nearby
they swoop so close to her head
I wonder if she will wake
tomorrow in terror, an inch shorter.
My dog is done sniffling
and we are both aware
nothing in our world has changed overnight.
I find comfort in these flashes;
a 6 A.M. bus, the crows, the cherry blossoms,
crocuses and maple buds.
And yes the robins that once
captured never leave.

Pasta Gardenia

Ingredients:

1 box fettuccini
1 bunch parsley fresh
1 box cherry tomatoes halved
1 pound fresh mushrooms
2 onions finely chopped

¼ cup apple cider vinegar
1/8 cup oil
½ cup Parmesan cheese

Directions:

• Boil water and then add fettuccine. Cook until tender.
• In a fry pan add one tablespoon oil. Sauté mushrooms and onions.
• When tender, add tomatoes and parsley.
• When pasta is cooked, drain and put back in pot.
• Add vegetables.
• Mix together oil and vinegar and add to mix.
• Top with Parmesan cheese and serve.

The Garden of My Wife
by Ron Charach, from *Selected Portraits,* Wolsak and Wynne, 2007

My wife wraps her long fingers with ferns
and tickles me with astilbe.
She cloaks the ground in periwinkle
and seamless green-white lamium.
The shade she feathers with dogwood,
ninebark, and spirea, greeting the morning
with day lilies in hot lemon, russet
and champagne.
Out front, columbines trumpet
the Japanese maple,
basking in light by wrought-iron
winding with Virginia creeper.
There is a more stately side.
Three mitred yews preside
over sculpted *sedum spectabile*
which softens the huge Muskoka rocks
that further widen
our cracked-stucco farmhouse
in the city.

What have I added?
A centurion row of hostas to slow the run-off
and a couple of globular yews
to hold court by the front door
alongside the burning bush?
Was I wrong to suppress her desire
for lush peonies and Annabelle hydrangea
even as I cheer her frail clematis
up wooden trellises
and wish her every rosebush well?
Her short-lived irises
more than once saved my life.

What a reluctant ornamental onion
in the garden I am, to say yes
to only two seedlings
when she always wanted three.

Back to Basics: Pasta with Legumes & Greens
Serves 2

Ingredients:

½ cup (125 mL) lentils, rinsed (green or red)
2 large, chopped onions
3 cloves garlic, sliced thin 1 teaspoon
2 tablespoons (30 mL) + 1 tablespoon (15 mL) olive oil
(5 mL) salt, divided into two parts
2 tablespoons (30 mL), or to taste, of chopped fresh rosemary (*or* parsley
or thyme)
4 cups (1 L) chopped kale
3 cups (750 mL) dried pasta, rotini OR fusilli, plain OR whole wheat
½ teaspoon (2 mL) ground nutmeg
¼ cup cranberries (optional)

Directions:

• Pour lentils and water into a saucepan. Bring to a boil, then reduce heat
and simmer gently for 15 to 20 minutes, or until tender, but not mushy.
• Remove from heat. Season with ½ teaspoon (2 mL) salt, and set aside.
• Heat 2 tablespoons (30 mL) olive oil in a large skillet or large saucepan.
• Add onion and cook, stirring constantly, for 1 minute. Reduce heat to low.
• Cover and cook, stirring occasionally, for 15 to 20 minutes, or until
onions are soft and moist.
• Uncover and increase heat to medium.
• Stir in remaining salt, garlic and rosemary (or parsley or thyme).
• Cook, stirring frequently, for 5 to 7 minutes, or until golden brown.

• Bring a large pot of salted water to boil.
• Add kale and bring back to a boil.
• Boil gently for 5 minutes, or until tender but not mushy.
• With tongs or a spoon, remove kale to a colander. Rinse with cold water
and drain thoroughly.

• Add lentils and their cooking liquid to the onions in the skillet.
• With scissors, cut boiled kale into smaller pieces as you add it to the
skillet.
• Add cooked pasta and enough of the cooking water to keep both pasta
and vegetables moist. Increase heat to high.
• Cook, and stir, until pasta is mixed in and heated through.

• Consider adding in the cranberries, for added colour and sweetness.

Cultural Cover
by Dianne Maguire

The acrid straw smell haunts
      the bright bursts of raffia
Sugar plum pink and orange
      Candy cane red and white
Stitched helter-skelter on
      Hats and mats and basketry
Set with shells
      And black-eyed John Crow beads
Piled and hung among Afro-Caribe carved masks
      and bowls stained to ebony.
Carmen Miranda dolls with island-naming aprons
      Sit watch over this veneer of culture,
The structure beneath,
      more substantial,
            yet unseen.

Rice and Peas

Rice and peas is a dish prepared on most Caribbean islands, but it is most associated with Jamaica.

Ingredients:

1 cup dried kidney beans or 1½ cups of canned red kidney beans
½ cup tinned coconut milk
1½ cups boiling salted water
1 tablespoon butter
1 small onion, chopped
1 cup uncooked white or brown rice
½ teaspoon of dried thyme
½ teaspoon
salt
A pinch of black pepper
¼ teaspoon of Pickapeppa sauce

Instructions:

• If using dried kidney beans, soak overnight, then boil in salted water until tender, about 1 hour.
• Drain the liquid into a measuring cup.
• Add the coconut milk and enough water to make 2 cups or 500 mL. Set the peas to one side. (If using canned kidney beans, drain the beans and use the liquid in the 2 cups.)
• Add the butter and onion, and cook until onion is clear.
• Then, add the rice, thyme, salt, black pepper and Pickapeppa sauce.
• Stir in the liquid and bring to a boil.
• Cover the pot and simmer until most of the liquid is absorbed (20 minutes).
• Add the cooked or canned peas and stir them in until evenly distributed through the partially cooked rice.
• Return the cover and cook until the rice has absorbed all the liquid and is tender (another 10 minutes).

Glowing
by Anthony Bansfield

words tingle in my mouth like habaneros
aflame with meaning, peppery in their intent
heated verses that no amount of liquid could quench

one scotch bonnet of a statement leaving sensations so stingingly perfect
they exclaim scalding rings of pain that inflame my gums
swell my lips, pulse a delicious agony throughout my body
and squeeze beads of perspiration down my face

squint my eyes with the intensity of vowels mouthed silently

a poetry so fiery that it causes me to gasp like an asthmatic

wheeze a silent J for jalapeño
scorching a trail of wordplay through my vocal array

blazing like a curry madras or njira torched with mitmita
with a grand finale featuring tamales and chillies
jerked to the point of tears, my sinuses drained, nostrils flared
from utterances best made only on a dare
choruses sprung from bottles with no labels
drop by drop of molten orange, basting taste buds in a blast furnace

deadly earnest, staining fingertips with indelible traces of sizzling lyrics

planting a pepperseed riddim in gardens of firebrands
who could season properly a stew of words so spiced

with life and love of degrees unknown

barometers blown

glowing

Calalloo, a stew, and one of my favourite dishes:

Ingredients:

¼ cup coconut milk
1 bunch calalloo bush (or spinach)
8 okras
6 green onions
¼ teaspoon pepper
1 teaspoon salt
2 cloves garlic, crushed
½ teaspoon vinegar

Directions:

• Grate coconut and extract cream (you can add a little water, stir it in a bowl, and squeeze small quantities of coconut at a time in a clean cloth).
• Wash and chop calalloo (or spinach) and green onions.
• In a saucepan, measure coconut milk and add 2 cups water.
• Combine with calalloo, okra, onions, pepper, salt and garlic.
• Bring to a boil and cook over medium heat till very soft and liquid is absorbed.
• Place in a blender and blend.
• Return to saucepan and keep hot till ready to serve.

Artichoke Hearts
by Carl Leggo

my cousin traded her grandmother's dark rum fruit cake recipe
with a neighbour for his pasta sauce with artichoke hearts,
and served the pasta to another neighbour who said,
That's the best pasta I've ever eaten, and now I want to eat you,
and for five or six winters dropped by for heart-to-heart tête-à-têtes
with tea and tea biscuits till another neighbour had a biscuit and cut to
the business of what in the world was going on since the neighbourhood
was reeling out of orbit like *Another World*

while my cousin knew, or pretended to know everybody in the small town
where everybody blows their car horns and waves like they haven't seen
you for years even though you just chatted about all the rain, snow, wind,
while shopping at Wal-Mart, and everybody stops to let you
into the stream of traffic even though there are no other cars anywhere,
and everybody knew, knew all about my cousin, except her husband
and nobody could tell him because everybody preferred to mind
their own business, everybody living the art of the choked heart

Pasta Sauce with Artichoke Hearts
(good with any kind of pasta)

Ingredients:

1 bottle (12 ounce), marinated artichoke hearts
¼ cup olive oil
2 cups onions, coarsely chopped
4 garlic cloves, finely chopped
1 cup fresh basil, chopped
½ teaspoon dried oregano
½ cup fresh parsley, finely chopped
½ teaspoon red pepper flakes
1 teaspoon black peppercorns, crushed
1 large can, diced tomatoes
1 teaspoon salt
⅓ cup Parmesan cheese, grated

Directions:

• Drain artichoke hearts and reserve marinade. Set both aside.
• Heat olive oil in a large saucepan and sauté onions, garlic, basil, oregano, parsley, and red pepper flakes over medium heat, 5 minutes.
• Add peppercorns, tomatoes, and salt, and simmer, uncovered, over medium heat for one hour.
• Remove some of the oil from the marinade, and add the rest of the marinade to the sauce.
• Simmer for 30 minutes.
• Cut artichoke hearts in half and add to the sauce.
• Simmer another 20 minutes.
• Add Parmesan before serving.

Desserts & Tea

Sensuous Peach
by Fern G. Z. Carr

Swaying on breaths
of sultry summer air,
peaches expose their cleavage

like the pendulous bosoms
of an exotic dancer
draped in a leafy boa.

I pluck a peach –
its velvet fuzz teases
my tongue;

droplets of nectar
spray with abandon
as I devour the blushing pulp,

juice trickles down my chin
and the taste of sweet flesh
satiates my desire.

Peach Crisp
Yields 6 servings

Fruit Base

3 x 14 ounce cans of sliced peaches
Few grains cinnamon
¼ cup white sugar

Topping

¼ cup margarine
½ cup flour
¾ cup brown sugar

• Melt margarine, then add flour and brown sugar.
• Combine until the mixture resembles large bread crumbs.
• Drain peaches well and place in a large bowl.
• Gently coat peaches with white sugar and cinnamon.
• Place peaches into a greased 8" x 8" glass baking dish.
• Sprinkle flour mixture on top of peaches to cover evenly.
• Bake at 350° F for 20 minutes until topping is crisp and brown.
• Serve with whipped topping if desired.

Love Flowing Forth
by Barbara Mary Frosch

One day my soul just opened up
and out poured so many
Wonderful thoughts and feelings
Tender loving ideas, tender loving gifts

Like tender young shoots
Reaching out from a new seed
To share with others, the perfume of light,
The truth of who I am.

For I am Love fully expressing,
Love trickles, then pours and cascades
Bubbling like a stream merrily meandering
Through meadows of flowers

Love flowing forth, touching all that it passes
Dancing, as sunlight from the heavens,
Reflects and sparkles on water,
Oh what a delight to let the sunlight of my soul
Light up the way of my everyday world.

Chocolate Tartlet "still warm and flowing on the inside" with a berry drizzle
Makes 4 cakes

Ingredients:

Berry Drizzle

150 g assorted berries (can be frozen)
25 g sugar
Juice and grind of ½ an organic lemon
Juice and grind of ½ an organic orange
3 tablespoons fruit liqueur

Tarts

80 g dark chocolate
170 g unsalted butter
1 tablespoon milk

1 vanilla pod
1 teaspoon ground cardamom
30 g white flour
50 g brown sugar
40 g finely ground almonds
The whites of 2 eggs

4 small high oven-forms
Butter to grease pans

Directions:

Berry Drizzle:

• Bring all ingredients, except the liqueur, to a boil in a sauce pan.
• Continue to cook berries on low heat for 3 minutes, till they become a soft mixture.
• Add liqueur.
• With a hand held blender, blend the mixture till it is a fine puree. Set aside and cool in fridge till serving.

Chocolate Tartlet
Preheat oven to 170° C

• Melt chocolate and butter in a pan over a warm water bath.
• Add and mix in milk, vanilla pod and cardamom.
• Take away from heat and stir in the flour, brown sugar and finely ground almonds.

• In another bowl, stiffly beat egg whites and gently fold into the chocolate mixture.
• Distribute the chocolate mixture evenly into the four well-greased forms.
• Place into the preheated oven and bake for about 20 minutes, or until they are just about done. The chocolate needs to be soft in the middle.

• Place the small forms on individual serving plates.
• Make a small incision in each tart and slowly pour some berry drizzle over the tart and some onto the plate.
• You may decorate the plate with a few fresh berries and mint leaves, or any other edible leaf or flower.
• Serve and enjoy immediately.

Erica's Song
by Andrew Tkach

From anointed king whom by lust grew bolder
To hapless swain by the stars crossing over
Even that artful imp of archers order
Could not have conceived of a beauty so true
No dear, in God's finest hour he let there be you

For you are to this world the lightening of days
In the hilt of your heart sweet refuge is made
Your soul is such you cast not shadow but shade
It is by grace that I've taken this view
And the risen Sun that's paying tribute to you

I proclaim, oh my love! Luminous and pure
Once held I floated like a ship tightly moored
With fluttering heart, as the dove that was lured
T'was like a dream and the dreams were too few
Although my greatest dream is to wake next to you

I forbear, as there's no end to your splendour!
And friendship comes first, I vow to remember
The sanctum of love is yours to surrender
If your name rose from the last breath I drew
Ere I leave this world I'd be singing, I love you

Angel Food Cake with Fresh Strawberries
(Adapted from Traditional Angel Food Cake)

Ingredients:

1¼ cups flour
1¾ cups white sugar or Xyla
¼ teaspoon salt
1½ cups egg whites
1 teaspoon cream of tartar
½ teaspoon almond extract
½ teaspoon vanilla extract
500 mL whipping cream (at least)
Strawberries, picked fresh

Instructions:

• Whip egg whites until they are stiff, then add cream of tartar, almond extract, and vanilla extract.
• Sift the flour, sugar, and salt together.
• Carefully stir the egg whites into the dry ingredients, then pour into an ungreased 10 inch tube pan.
• Place the cake pan into the oven. Turn the oven on to 325° F and bake for about an hour, until it is golden brown.
• Remove it from the oven, turn it upside down and let it cool down in the dish.
• Wash the fresh strawberries. Cut out the stems and slice them. Chill in the fridge.
• Sprinkle strawberries with Xyla or Stevia to taste.
• Pour the cream into a bowl. Add in a teaspoon of vanilla extract. Whip with an electric beater until it becomes thick.
• Remove the pan and serve cake with fresh strawberries topped with whipped cream.

Rainbows & More
by: Melvina Germain

I've been walking under the arch of rainbows,
quenched with lemon juice,
bathed with the falling rain.
I've been in the now with every step I take,
mellowed with a sip of tea
and a huge piece of rainbow cake,
that slowly enters my mouth
creating a sensual dance with my tongue.
O I've been Blessed in this universe
to walk against the wind,
wrapped with the morning sun,
kissed by mother nature.
I've been many places,
trudging on soft sand
as it massages my feet so gently.
Standing at the river's edge
watching the eddies play,
and skipping stones in the afternoon of the day.
Yes I'm elated, intoxicated and drunk
with the beauty of this world.
As I dance and twirl
with my palms held toward the sky,
I say, someday, come and walk with me
by your side.

Simple Rainbow Four Layer Cake

Ingredients:

2 boxes of Betty Crocker Super Moist White Cake mix
4 tins of Betty Crocker icing sugar, tightened up with 2 heaping tablespoon
of powder icing sugar per tin
3 boxes of Smarties, take out the brown Smarties
4 tubes of food dye (Red, Blue, Yellow and Green)
"Red & Blue" makes purple

Directions:

• Mix batter as specified by the instructions on the box.
• Separate batter into 4 equal parts.
• Colour each part as you wish. My colours are yellow, purple, pink and
green.
• Grease and flour each pan so the cake doesn't stick to the sides of the
pan.
• Bake in four 8 inch round baking pans, the specified time.

• Take from oven and cool on a rack, then place wax paper over each layer.
• Place in a plastic bag and freeze for easier icing.
• Take icing from tins, add icing powder and mix well to a nice thick
consistency so it holds on the cake and does not run.
• Ice the first layer and place the second on top, ice top and sides, take
the third and fourth and repeat until the whole cake is covered with white
icing.

• You will need a decorating tool to make very simple rosettes with the
leftover icing to go around the bottom of the cake. I mixed a little of the
blue food colour.
• Fill tool and set aside.

• Empty all Smarties into a small bowl and place all over the cake using all
three packages.
• Decorate the bottom of the cake with the blue rosettes.

• Cake is ready for your party or afternoon ladies' tea.
• Great for kids' parties
• Enjoy your rainbow cake.

My Muse Refused to Visit
by Susan J. Atkinson

despite offers
of scones and tea

perhaps I expected
too much
a reply to my
hospitality?

but she had no interest

and even when
the offer changed
to champagne
and berries bursting
with summer

she was a no show

my muse refused
to be lured
though I was prepared
to lay out any delicacy
to satisfy her whim

instead I caught her
arm in arm
with someone new

someone who had only to offer
water and bread.

Evening Scones
Makes 8 scone wedges.

2 cups sifted all-purpose flour
1 tablespoon baking powder
2 tablespoons sugar
½ teaspoon salt
¼ cup shortening
2 eggs
⅓ cup heavy cream
1 tablespoon sugar

• Sift together flour, baking powder, 2 tablespoons sugar and salt into mixing bowl.
• Cut in shortening until mixture resembles coarse meal or crumbs.
• Make a hollow in the center.

• Set aside 1 tablespoon egg white for topping.
• Beat remaining eggs: combine with cream and add all at once to hollow in flour mixture.
• Stir only enough to mix – the dough will be stiff.

• Turn dough onto lightly floured board and knead lightly 5 or 6 times, or until dough sticks together.
• Divide in half.
• Roll each half to make a 6 inch circle about 1 inch thick.
• Cut each circle into 4 wedges.

• Arrange wedges about 1 inch apart on ungreased baking sheet.
• Brush tops with reserved egg white; sprinkle with 1 tablespoon sugar.

• Bake in oven at 400° F for about 15 minutes, or until golden brown.
• Serve at once.

• For a variation add ½ cup raisins, dried cranberries or dried blueberries.

Best served with a nice cup of tea, clotted cream and sweet summer berries!

Elan Vital
by Cynthia Sharp

In the movement of pastry through fingers,
the plenty that prevails even in hardship,
my Godson measures earnestly,
his three-year-old palms
rolling and shaping with such concentration,
I ponder if he can even fathom
how much he is loved,
while in requiescence and remembrance,
my grandmother's hands
sift the gifts of the Earth
into pastries and pies
through my own.

My Granny's Raisin Pie

Ingredients:

1 tablespoon white sugar
¼ cup water at room temperature
¾ cup brown sugar
2½ tablespoons white flour
1½ cups raisins
¼ cup cold water
1 teaspoon vanilla
2 tablespoons butter

Directions:

• In a medium-sized pot, brown white sugar until it is light brown.
• Shake the pot. Do not burn!
• Remove from heat. Add ¼ cup water at room temperature.
• Put back onto heat until the sugar dissolves in the water.

• Mix brown sugar and white flower in bowl.
• Add in raisins and cold water. Mix again.
• Add the mixture to the pot.
• Stir and cook on low heat for 15 minutes, stirring occasionally to prevent sticking.
• Remove from heat and stir in vanilla and butter.

• Pour into an unbaked 9 inch pastry shell.
• Add top crust and seal edges.
• Brush pastry (not the edges) with pastry brush dipped in milk.
• Sprinkle with a tiny amount of white sugar.
• Cut 4-5 slits ¼ inch in diameter in the top centre of pie.
• Bake pie at 425° F for 10 minutes, on the lowest oven rack.
• Reduce heat to 350° F and bake for an additional 20 minutes.
• Remove when edges are dark and cool.
• Enjoy!

Beaver Pond
by Jeffrey Mackie

Newspaper talks to me
Television interrupts.
Clipping parts of my life
To tape to the wall
All my hope
Has been downloaded
And I can't remember where
I saved it.

Gone is the forest
And the beaver pond
Where we played hockey
As children
It is houses now
And a street called Walden.

Generations before ours
Lost so much more
But we learned to cry
Into the camera
Into the microphone.

Should I grind fair trade coffee
Or drink Nescafe,
What is more authentic today?
You, Me
Discount Distractions
Cultural ADD.

Mom's Traditional Scuffles

Ingredients:

1 package yeast
¼ cup lukewarm water
3 cups flour
½ teaspoon salt
3 tablespoons sugar
1 cup butter
½ cup milk
2 eggs
¼ cup sugar and cinnamon

Directions:

• Combine yeast and lukewarm water. Let stand a few minutes.
• Mix: flour, salt, 3 tablespoons sugar and butter.
• Add: milk, 2 eggs, and the yeast mixture.
• Knead 'til soft. Leave, covered, overnight in fridge.
• Divide into four parts. Roll each part out on a layer of about ¼ cup sugar and cinnamon.
• Cut into approximately 1.5 inch wide wedges (triangles) and roll up from wide end.
• Bake 15 minutes in 350° F oven.

The dough can be frozen, the scuffles can be frozen, all sorts of things can be done to prevent you from eating the entire batch right away. I recommend having friends around when you make them, so that you cannot eat them all yourself.

Soap Bubbles
by Daisuke Kinoshita

Life is like soap bubbles.

Life seems to be long,
but it is short.
We have no time to belong
where we don't want.

We are so weak.
We are easily blown away.
But we are born to seek
a place to fly away to.

Find a place that you can shine on.

Canadian Style Bubble Tea for Two
(Adapted from Classic Bubble Tea)

Ingredients:

½ cup dried boba tapioca pearls
2 tea bags
1 cup almond milk
¾ cup white sugar
maple syrup to taste
water

Directions:

• Cook the Boba – 4 cups of water for every ½ cup of boba:
• Cook on high until the water boils.
• Add in the boba bubbles and stir gently until they begin floating to the top of the water.
• Turn the heat to medium and cook the boba for 15 minutes.
• Remove the pan from heat, cover, and let the pearly bubbles sit for another 15 minutes.

Create syrup for the pearly bubbles:

• Bring 1 cup of water to a boil over high heat.
• Remove from heat and stir in ¾ cup sugar until dissolved.
• Set the mixture aside to cool.
• Make two strong cups of tea in large glasses.
• Leaving lots of room for bubbles and almond milk.
• Chill them in the fridge.
• Drain the boba from any residual water and pour the syrup over top. Refrigerate for at least 20 minutes.
• Now, your pearly bubbles are ready for their destination!
• Remove the tea from the fridge and add in the bubbles!
• Follow with almond milk and sweeten to taste with maple syrup.
• On hot days, crush ice into glasses and pour the bubble tea over the ice.

Bubble tea is best served right away!

sunset
by Tara Wohlberg

when the sun sets west
feathered shift of sky
satin clouds undress
Heaven's kiss bids the flat light good-bye

endless calm   red mist
glistening golden beams
gently they are kissed
by night's dark melting blaze of dreams

Flapper Pie

This old prairie pie prevents you from ever getting into a flap over dessert!

Ingredients:

Crust
1¼ cups graham wafer crumbs
⅓ cup melted butter

Custard
3 cups whole milk
¾ cup sugar
4½ tablespoons corn starch dissolved in a little of the cold milk from the 3 cups
pinch of salt
3 eggs, separated

Meringue
4½ additional tablespoons sugar for the egg whites
1½ tablespoons butter
1½ teaspoons vanilla

Instructions
• Preheat your oven to 350° F. Mix crumbs with melted butter. Set aside ¼ cup for topping. Use a glass to press crumbs firmly into pie plate. Build sides up high so your custard doesn't spill over. Bake 15 minutes. Remove and cool.
• Whisk egg yolks in a small bowl. Set aside.
• Heat milk in a large saucepan. Add the sugar and a pinch of salt, and whisk until dissolved. Slowly add the corn starch/milk mixture and continue to whisk until the mixture (over medium heat) starts to thicken. Whisk for a few minutes more to cook the corn starch.
• Whisk in the egg yolks and continue to whisk until the mixture becomes very thick. This should just take 2-3 minutes. Don't have the heat too high or you'll burn your custard. Take it off the heat and whisk in butter and vanilla. Pour into crumb pie shell.
• Using a mixer, add egg whites and whisk until foamy. Slowly add sugar, a tablespoon or so at a time. Whisk egg whites until stiff and glossy.
• Spread whipped egg whites over the custard, making sure they cover ALL the custard right to the edges.
• Sprinkle the ¼ cup of crumbs over the top. Place on centre of middle rack in oven. Bake at 350° F for 12 to 15 minutes until golden brown. Cool at room temperature and then pop in the refrigerator 1-2 hours to set

custard. This pie should be eaten the day it is made, as custard weeps when it is stored in the refrigerator. But weeping or not, it is still good the next day – no use crying over a pie…

Contributor Biographies

Susan J. Atkinson is a poet, children's writer and Kindergarten teacher. Her hobbies include enjoying the accomplishments of her four daughters, running long distances and making up stories for TV with her filmmaker husband.

Anthony Bansfield, the nth digri, is inspired by his Caribbean and Canadian heritage, hip-hop culture, and the African griot tradition. He produced WordLife, a poetry and music compilation that marked the emerging African Canadian spoken word movement and co-founded the Canadian Festival of Spoken Word, the first national slam poetry tournament in Canada.

Wendy Bullen Stephenson has a PhD from the Department of Curriculum Studies at UBC and has hosted almost 100 international students. Her original recipe, vegetarian frittata, appears in the March #5 diary entry of her online, imaged novel, *Vancouver Memories: My Year Abroad*. It is the peace offering that Sandford serves to Erika at a picnic in the snow in Stanley Park.

Fern G. Z. Carr is a member of The League of Canadian Poets who composes and translates poetry in five languages. A 2013 Pushcart Prize nominee, she has been published extensively from Finland to the Seychelles and had her work recognized by the Parliamentary Poet Laureate.

Ron Charach is a psychiatrist/poet who lives in Toronto. He is the author of nine books of poetry, most recently, *Forgetting the Holocaust*.

Caroline de Chavigny was born and raised in Montreal, where she received her Bachelor of Science with an emphasis in business. She currently lives in the southwestern United States. Her desire to help people was the catharsis that led to her series of children's books, as well as the inspirational novel, *When Angels Die*.

Teresa-Lee (Terry) Cooke lives in Winnipeg, Manitoba, with her partner Wes and two feline folk. TLC is a member of the Manitoba Writers' Guild and The Writers Collective of Manitoba. She likes to write poetry that can be presented as "spoken word." Teresa-Lee writes in hope that you can relate to her journey…we are all connected.

Barbara Frosch is a singer and poet who has been published in *Island Skies*, a compilation of Canadian poetry. She is currently working on a new book, *Enlightening the Souls.* Barbara has starred in several roles in musical theatre and was delighted to find new passion while singing with the Edmonton Opera.

Melvina Germain, born in Sydney, Nova Scotia, validates and exemplifies how diversity is the diamond chip of poetic success. Her perpetual passion and yen for broadening her literary scope has enabled her to establish herself as a solid multi-style poet.

David Helwig was born in Toronto in 1938. He now lives in a village in Prince Edward Island. He has published many volumes of poetry, fiction and nonfiction. His most recent collection of poetry is *Seawrack* (Frog Hollow Press).

Daisuke Kinoshita works in tourism in British Columbia, where he lives with his lovely wife Miwa. His first collection of poetry has been celebrated for its elegant beauty. He has been a featured reader at Cradle Our Spirit Healer's Guild events.

Rogr Lee is from British Columbia, where he now works as a picture framer. Previously, Rogr spent many years in Toronto playing and writing music in a vibrant song-writing scene there. He now periodically paints and records at home.

Carl Leggo is a poet and professor at the University of British Columbia. His books include: *Come-By-Chance*; *Teaching to Wonder: Responding to Poetry in the Secondary Classroom*; and *Sailing in a Concrete Boat: A Teacher's Journey.*

Jeffrey Mackie is an internationally published and translated poet. A prolific performer, many of his readings can be seen on YouTube. Mackie also does literary journalism, contributing interviews and reviews to various media in Montreal.

Dianne Maguire is a Jamaican-born Canadian writer who lives in Vancouver. Her thesis for her MA in Creative Writing from UBC is a published collection of short stories set in Jamaica, *Dryland Tourist*. She has had poems published, and won prizes in literary contests. In recent years, she has been working on articles, activities and novels for her ESL students.

rob mclennan is the author of more than twenty trade books of poetry, fiction and non-fiction. He won the John Newlove Poetry Award in 2010, and was longlisted for the CBC Poetry Prize in 2012. He and his wife Christine recently welcomed newborn daughter Rose into the world.

Wendy Morris has a passion for Holistic Health, especially aromatherapy and energy healing. In addition to being a business owner of a Natural Product Store and full time Massage Clinic, she finds time to make organic soaps, creams and essential oil formulas, as well as to write several blogs and articles for a natural health magazine.

Marc Mullo was born, raised, and still resides in Thunder Bay. He's been a part-time poet and freelancer for over twelve years, despite depression and other extenuating circumstances. His work has been published with the Poetry Institute of Canada. He also has a book, *Poetic Potpourri.*

Bonnie Nish is founder and Executive Director of Pandora's Collective Outreach Society in Vancouver and Executive Producer of the Summer Dreams Literary Arts Festival. She has a Masters in Arts Education and is currently pursuing a PhD in Expressive Arts Therapy at the European Graduate School. Her first book of poetry, *Love and Bones,* is available at Karma Press.

Honey Novick is a singer/songwriter/voice teacher/poet. A full member of the League of Canadian Poets, she lives in Toronto and survived the Ice Storm and Polar Vortex.

Nicole Scoffield is a freelance musician who sings and fiddles with *The Wheat In The Barley.* She has a solo CD, *Colouring,* and teaches violin from her private studio in Vancouver, BC.

Cynthia Sharp has been published in *Lantern Magazine, Toasted Cheese, Haiku Journal, 50 Haikus & Three Line Poetry* and was nominated for the *Pushcart Prize & Best of the Net Anthology.* She enjoys the beauty of nature on the west coast, where she is at work on a series of fantasy novels for tweens and teens.

Andrew Tkach began writing poetry as a teen struggling with bipolar, attempting to make sense of the great storm within. His novella, *Sentries of Heaven,* can be found on Facebook. A student of acting, Andrew currently resides in North Vancouver, B.C.

Tara Wohlberg is a poet, lyricist and freelance writer. Her lyrics are published by EC Schirmer, Boston, and Oxford University Press. Her work has been short-listed for the *Malahat Review Open Season* award and recently appeared in *CV2* and *Quills.* Her chapbook, *Cold Surely Takes the*

Wood, was published by Alfred Gustav Press, in spring, 2013.

40301565R00040

Made in the USA
Charleston, SC
02 April 2015